HISTORY
in a
HURRY

Ancient
China

written and drawn by
JOHN FARMAN

MACMILLAN
CHILDREN'S BOOKS

First published 1998 by Macmillan Children's Books
a division of Macmillan Publishers Limited
25 Eccleston Place, London SW1W 9NF
and Basingstoke

Associated companies throughout the world

ISBN 0 330 37087 1

Text and illustrations copyright © John Farman 1998

1 3 5 7 9 8 6 4 2

A CIP catalogue record for this book is available from
the British Library.

Printed and bound in Great Britain
by Mackays of Chatham plc, Kent

☁ CONTENTS

🕊 *OFF WE GO!*

What do you think of when you hear the word China?

Take-away food, amazing dragon parades, chopsticks and rice, high-pitched squeaky music and back-to-front upside-down writing?

Well, there's a lot more to China than that.* It's a massive country with the highest population in the world (and growing), an incredible history and an unpredictable future. One of the reasons that we seem to know so little about them

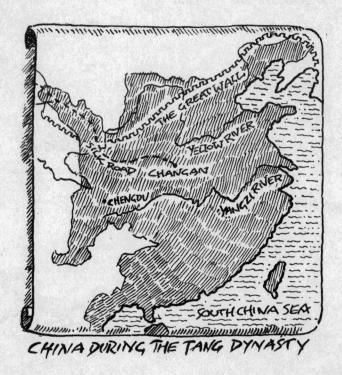

CHINA DURING THE TANG DYNASTY

*You amaze me. Ed

is that from way, way back in antiquity, the Chinese have, until relatively recently, kept themselves very much to themselves, staying as far away as possible from all the pointless in-fighting that the rest of the world inflicts upon itself.

Within the pages of this lavishly illustrated and staggeringly comprehensive volume, I'll try and tell you all you need to know about a highly sophisticated society that was flourishing at a time when we were still grovelling around in the mud being Ancient Britons.

By the way, if you're wondering what those grumpy little comments at the bottom of the pages are, it's my editor, Susie, telling me off. Please ignore them.

🗨️ Chapter 1

🗨️ THE HISTORICAL BIT

Ages ago (to be not very precise), small groups of people began settling in the Yellow River Valley where China is now. The soil, they discovered, was so fertile that they only had to wave a seed at it and it would grow. Having said that, it wasn't all plain sailing (or even farming), as this area was also prone to severe draughts,* even worse floods and lots of horrid earthquakes. The Chinese soon realized it was pretty darn important to stay mates with nature, so they worshipped and made sacrifices to it – a sort of ecological insurance policy.

The valley farmers multiplied and gradually spread south into the Yangtse River Valley and the West River Valley, cos the weather down south was better, and by 1500 BC the Chinese had got themselves a mighty kingdom, mostly farmland but with an ever-increasing number of towns and villages.

Who's Who . . . and When?
The throne in Ancient China got passed down from father to son of a particular family, before said family was kicked out for a new one. These families and the period in which they ruled are called 'dynasties'.

*Do you mean 'droughts'? Ed

Very briefly, the history of China went like this:

5000 BC: Early farmers set up in the Yellow River Valley.
2852 BC: The beginning of the reigns of the nine legendary emperors (I could list them but they all sound the same to me).
2200 BC: Hsia dynasty
1500 BC: Shang dynasty
1027 BC: Chou dynasty
481 BC: A period when all the states were at war.
256 BC: Ch'in dynasty
206 BC: Han dynasty
AD 220: The period of the Six Dynasties begins.

So when was Ancient China?

As you can see from the above, it covers an incredibly long time, so just to give you an idea of how things worked, we'll glance at one of the most important dynasties – the Han dynasty (206 BC to AD 220).

Chapter 2

HANGING OUT WITH 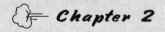 THE HANS

Wall-to-Wall

What the Hans were most famous for was joining up all the bits of the Great Wall of China into one. These bits of wall had been built over the centuries to stop the ever-increasing threat from Asiatic nomads and also to act as a base for the Chinese to push the invading Huns (not to be confused with Hans) back north where they belonged.

There had been a series of terrible famines in Central Asia and the weather had turned really nasty, so everyone who could move . . . did. Just imagine it, there you were, a poor, chilly and hungry Hun, trudging slowly across a mighty plain of pure nothingness, trying desperately to find a more hospitable (and hopefully darn sight warmer) place to set up, when, all of a sudden, right in front of you, stretching as far as your tired eyes can see in either direction, there's a socking great wall.* Weird or what?

Keep Out!

So when these poorly fed, fed-up folk arrived at this massive wall, they probably got the message that the Chinese weren't that wild on them going much further east. Reluctantly, they all sloped off to the West instead. The Great Migration, as it

*It couldn't have been longer than this sentence. Ed

D'YOU THINK THEY'RE TRYING TO TELL US SOMETHING?

was called, finally brought them face to face with the ever-growing Roman Empire, leading to the collision which would eventually bring the whole lot (the Roman lot, that is) tumbling down.

Who's Chou?

The dynasty before the one before Han was called the Chou dynasty and during this period a pattern built up that would set the way things were to be for hundreds of years. The noblemen, who'd been given whole districts to rule by the king (who they never listened to anyway), had become extremely uppity, fighting over land all the time. These districts became known as the Warring States. This made life very tough for your run-of-the-mill peasant – who died in his thousands, never knowing from one minute to the next whose side he was supposed to be on, let alone who he belonged to (sounds like a bit like the Liberal Democrats).

Confucius Rules

Some smart people tried to make things better by following the ideas of a certain Confucius (551–479 BC), a wise old philosopher and famous clever person, who travelled round the country (not a small job in big China) begging everyone to be loyal (especially to the king), to obey their parents and to generally be as nice as poss. The noblemen, who were having a ball without these silly new ideas, thought he was a bit of a nerd, and made their local laws even stricter and punishments even nastier. These chaps were called *legalists* (amongst other things!). Later, when Confucius' followers began to get the best jobs in the central government, the legalists had to listen – or else! Eventually old Confucius was regarded as the best person that ever lived (until Elvis, of course) and was worshipped in temples all over the Chinese Empire.

Lao Tzu

Lao Tzu, the other great eastern philosopher, lived at around about the same time as Confucius but was much older. He thought that all governments were pretty pointless as they always ended up making a mess of things (sound familiar?), and that anyone who dressed up for ceremonies was downright silly. Lao Tzu told his followers that they should ignore governments (smart move) and go back to the simple life, just obeying the laws of nature. This was called Taoism, and has become rather trendy these days.

In the end, Lao Tzu, seeing the way the country was going, got fed up with banging his wise old head against the wall (probably the Great Wall) and upped and left. Luckily, one of the guards of the pass that led out of China persuaded the old crosspatch to leave one of his books behind and, I'm pleased to report, it is from this very book that the whole Taoist movement began.

Useless Fact No. 622
No one has a clue what happened to old Lao. (Or even if he actually existed.)

Meanwhile . . .
Back to the plot. By AD 213, the Chinese couldn't tolerate the goody-goody Confucian way of life and the First Emperor of the new Ch'in (pronounced *sin*) Dynasty, Shih Huang Ti, decided to burn all books. The scholars who didn't go along with this (it's a bit tricky being a scholar without books) were buried alive (about 450 of 'em) – which seemed to do the trick.

Anyone for Eternal Life?
The real reason for Shih's severely short temper was the fact that the scholars and alchemists had failed to come up with the much sought-after Elixir of Life which, once swallowed, meant you could live for ever (beats lager!). Searching for this old elixir had become a bit of an obsession throughout the world in the Middle Ages.

Despite the book burning, it was during Shih Huang Ti's rule that China became mighty and strong. Instead of the awful noblemen, the Emperor sent out his own proper civil servants to rule the far-flung districts with an iron glove (well, a few iron gloves, actually). He built a wonderful network of roads and waterways, finished off the Great Wall, standardized weights and measures and, best of all, made sure that everyone used the same sort of writing (fat lot of good that must've been – with no books).

The Plot Thickens
When First Emperor and top tyrant Shih died (aged 49) whilst out and about searching for that blasted elixir (obviously too late), his chief minister, Li Si, and the eunuch, Zhao Gao, decided not to tell anyone, cos they didn't want his first son, the honourable Fu Su, to be emperor.

Li and Zhao sent a forged letter from the dead Emperor to his son Fu, ordering him to commit suicide, which he did. Obedient, in those days, weren't they!

Trouble was, the journey back to the capital was long and hot and the old Emperor's body started to go off – causing everywhere they passed through to stink to high heaven. The minister rather cleverly arranged to have a carriage of rotting fish follow his dead master's carriage so that nobody would smell a rat (or a dead Emperor). I think I might just have wondered just why there was a carriage of rotten fish in the Emperor's procession, but then I always was suspicious. Anyway, the whole scam worked out fine and the dead Emperor's second son, the totally useless and bullyable Hu Hai, got the throne. Hey ho.

Everything went well until Zhao Gao (the eunuch) ratted on Li Si (the minister) and somehow got him executed, before forcing the Second Emperor (Hu Hai) to kill himself (Ho Ho). He (Zhao Gao) was going for the top job himself (moral: never trust a eunuch). However, the Chinese didn't think much of having a eunuch (see Useless Fact below) as emperor, and his plan was thwarted.

The new Emperor only lasted a few months, and in 206 BC rebel armies knocked down the front door of the Imperial Palace and promptly massacred all the occupants before burning the city of Xianyang to the ground.

Useless Fact No. 623
Eunuchs were male palace servants and guards who had had all their – how should I say – 'tackle' removed, to make sure that they couldn't get up to any funny business with the emperors' wives or servants.*

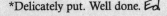

*Delicately put. Well done. Ed

Poor but Honest

In the colossal bunfight between all the rebel factions that followed, the Han family (Confucians) came out top in 206 BC with their best lad, known as Han Gaozu, starring as emperor. Coming from the poor side of the family, he turned out to be ever so nice and kind, scrapping a whole lot of horrid laws (apart from those involving murder and violence). He then let the scholars have their books back and even listened to what they had to say. He also did away with slavery and the suffering of the very, very poor, instituting an early form of famine relief.

72 Not Out

Han Gaozu was a remarkable-looking man by all accounts, with an unusually long prominent nose, a huge forehead and 72 black moles on his left thigh, supposed to prove his supernatural status. I've got a few on my back – I wonder what that proves.

Hat Alert

Gaozu wasn't always easy to get on with. He hated pomp and ceremony and on one occasion, when some of the scholars turned up in ridiculously elaborate outfits, he promptly snatched one of their well-over-the-top articles of headgear and urinated in it.

Everyone thought Gaozu was really fab (except perhaps the guy whose hat it was), even the civil servants called mandarins (like those little oranges?) who ran the states for him.* The only ones that weren't that thrilled were the dreadful noblemen who had made living in China so frightfully tedious for so long.

*How could a little orange run a state? Ed

Useless Fact No. 627

Mandarins were to become very important in ancient China. You could tell 'em apart by the different colours they were allowed to wear, and the various animals and birds that adorned their wonderful clothes.

Cool-School

Suddenly everyone could go to school and university and people were employed for how clever they were rather than how rich their family was. Gaozu sent off Chang Ch'ien, his top soldier, westwards, to take a peek at the outside world and see if he could rustle up any trade. The first swap they did was silk for horses.

Useless Fact No. 630

The Chinese, at that time, only had rather little and rather slow mountain ponies. They wanted the big, fast, sports models that came from Asia.

The Silk Road

Much later, the famous Silk Road, which stretched from the salt lake, Lop Nor, right through to Tashkent in Russia one way, and the mighty city of Kashgar in Turkistan in the other, developed as the main route through to the West for the long camel and oxen trains carrying China's exports, especially silk. It was along the Silk Road (in the other direction) that Buddhism, which was to become the main religion, first crept into China.

In addition to travelling overland, huge ocean-going junks began to sail further and further afield, bartering silk and gold for pearls, glass and all the other stuff they didn't have at home (which is, I suppose, the main point of trade). Eventually, China was swapping their gear for just about everything from pomegranates to pizzas all over the Middle East and as far afield as Greece and Iran.

Useless Fact No. 631

Getting to where they wanted to go was made easier by the invention of the rudder – around AD 210.

LEFT, RIGHT, LEFT AGAIN, AND STRAIGHT ON

The Golden Age

In 140 BC the 14-year-old Emperor Wu Di became host to what was later called the Golden Age. His fantastic army finally put paid to the pesky Huns and Tartars using powerful new-fangled rockets and gunpowder (before it had only been used for fireworks or shooing off evil spirits).

Wu Di doubled the size of the empire during his reign but didn't want to share it with the nobility, which annoyed them big-time as they preferred the sort of royalty who kept their noses out of the running of the country (like ours do – usually). Wu took this further and any official who even began to show vague signs of possibly becoming a bit powerful, was accused of some trumped-up crime and removed (well, at least his head was). If anyone even began to criticise Wu they were for the chop, even though his economic policies were rapidly sliding the country down the pan.

Officially Confused

He did, however, state that Confucianism should be the recognized cult in 136 BC and woe betide anyone who opposed it. He set up an Imperial University in Chang'an for 'great scholars' to examine and interpret the five Confucian classics (too long to list*).

Chaos

Chinese history is nothing if not predictable: as soon as something begins to settle down, chaos comes galloping in to break it all up again. So, around AD 8, a young prince called Wang Mang set to and undid all of Wu Di's good work, destroying his excellent administration and bringing back the

*There's only five! Ed

very worst aspects of feudalism. Money lost all its value because forgeries flooded the markets and, worse still, the dreaded Huns started bashing away at the borders again.

Test (to be completed without looking)
Who were:

1. Chou?
2. Lao Tzu?
3. Shi Huang Ti?
4. Erh Huang Ti?
5. Zhua Gao?
6. Li Si?
7. Fu Su?
8. Hu Hui?
9. Han Gaozu?
10. Chang Ch'en?
11. Wu Di?
12. Wang Mang?
13. Hu Cares?

 **Chapter 3**

THE EVER-SO-CLEVER
 CHINESE

Home on the Range

Physically the Chinese Empire grew so huge that trying to describe the conditions for farming is a bit pointless, as you might have come across everything from sopping water meadows to blistering deserts and still be in China. Just to make what water they had go further, they built a whole load of canals and irrigation channels. The south got far more rain (most of the time they were up to their knees in it) – which turned out to be great for growing rice. Up north they grew

ANOTHER CHINESE FIRST

mulberry trees for feeding the silkworms that the Chinese women could later unravel to produce fine thread for their clothes, and wheat and millet (for feeding their budgies*).

The countryside was divided up a bit like the feudal system that hit Europe much later. The farmer was given a piece of land by whoever was in charge – that was the good news. The bad news was that he had to give back a daftly high proportion of whatever he grew. As if this wasn't enough, the poor old farm person was expected to spend one month a year on whatever took the boss's fancy – road building and mending, crop gathering, building fortresses or going to fight the odd war – you get the picture.

Good Ideas

As I mentioned earlier, nature was really important to the early Chinese and they learned ever such a lot from it, especially from the weather and the sky. By the end of the Han dynasty they'd developed loads of brilliant instruments to study and measure such things. Most important was the magnetic compass, thought up by the Hans and developed by the T'angs.

Way Ahead

The Chinese turned out to be much much cleverer than us lot over in the West and reached a level of civilization that we could only dream about.

- All the cities had walls around them and massive forts to protect the occupants.
- Their magnificent temples were even flasher than the ones the Romans had.

*They didn't have budgies. Ed

三 They had carriages and horses with proper harnesses (so they could pull things without throttling themselves).

四 They had huge boats in which they sailed the seven seas.

五 They had spinning wheels so they could run up nice little frocks to wear.

六 They invented gunpowder, so they could blow their enemies and each other limb from limb and, best of all . . .

七 They invented paper and ink – so they could write and tell each other how clever they were.

Useless Fact No. 633
In AD 105, paper was invented by mandarin Ts'ai Lun on account of silk being too expensive to write all his many letters on.

Iron for Ages
The Iron Age proper hit China before the West and by the Han Dynasty the digging-up of iron and copper by the zillions of

slaves was really big business. Around the mines, towns grew up with foundries, cooling tanks, furnaces, large pits for storage and, of course, living quarters for the workers. These 'factories' not only produced day-to-day tools made out of metal, they also churned out millions of weapons – from arrowheads to spears to swords (and all the fiddly little metal bits on crossbows), as well as helmets and armour.

Iron gradually took over from bronze for most things, but bronze continued to be used for coins and mirrors, the massive bells for the temples and all the other stuff like vases and incense-burners for the ceremonies.

*(In case you haven't worked it out yet,
the symbols used below are the
Chinese numbers 1-10)**

A Few Ancient Chinese Firsts

➤ 7000 BC. Pig alert! The Chinese were the first to try eating them. Sausages came later. There are still more pigs in China than in the rest of the world.

➤ 3000 BC. Tea! Emperor Shang Cheng was sitting in his garden one afternoon when a couple of leaves blew off a nearby bush and fell in his cup. They apparently made his hot water taste funny but rather pleasant.

➤ 2700 BC. Mrs Huang-ti, an emperor's wife, spent many hours of her time taking the little silk coats off little worms, tying them together and making them into big silk coats for herself.

四 2000 BC. Acupuncture began. See Chapter 9.

*Are you sure they're right? Ed
I sure hope so! JF

WHERE IS THIS PARK OF INTELLIGENCE?

— SEARCH ME!

五 1900 BC. How to pamper a panda. Put him in a nice, new zoo. The Chinese built the very first zoo in the Park of Intelligence in Peking.

六 1300 BC. Lacquer was discovered. The first natural plastic. The Chinese worked out that by tapping the bark of the *Rhus verniciflua* tree it would give up a kind of sticky liquid, that when dry could hardly be damaged by anything. They used it to coat their dishes as a cheap alternative to the rich man's bronze ones.

七 1270 BC. The sundial was invented. Some clever Chinese person, called Zhou Kung, was trying to work out what time it was, and stuck a post in the ground to see where the shadow fell. Hey presto! it was a quarter past three. Unfortunately, it didn't work that well in the dark.

八 1000 BC. If you're wondering why some Chinese people's eyes are so narrow, it could be from sucking lemons: they were the first to cultivate them.

九 200 BC. The umbrella seems so obvious but, like all things, someone had to invent it. The Chinese did just that. It was brought to these shores by the traveller Sir Jonas Hongway in 1700 and something.*

千 100 BC. The Chinese discovered that blood circulates round their bodies before anyone else (who wants second-hand blood?).

(I only know as far as 10, so we'll have to start again . . .)

一 AD 100. The compass was discovered. Interestingly enough, the needle only pointed south, which must have been a right problem if they wanted to go north.

二 AD 105. The Chinese made the first proper paper and bamboo pens – but what to write with? No problemo. They'd already made the first ink out of smoke and glue and aromatic substances in 2500 BC.

三 AD 400. If you ever want to blame someone for ironing, try the Chinese. They used a brass contraption filled with hot coals to smooth their clothes.

四 AD 700. The very first arched bridge (arches give extra strength) was invented by engineer Li-Chun. The Chinese were also the first to build the suspension bridge.

五 Language! Chinese is the only ancient language still in use, and is the main link between China's thousand million population.

*Could you be a bit more precise? Ed
No. JF

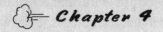

Chapter 4

GODS, DEATH AND
= ALL THAT

The Chinese, like many other early civilizations, believed that throughout their land, in the trees, the mountains, the rivers, the seas, the air, the rain and the wind, lived loads of spirits that needed keeping happy – or else!

Or else, there'd be floods, earthquakes, eclipses and droughts. They were, therefore, always offering them valuable presents, animal sacrifices or food, through special in-between people called 'shamans' who claimed they were real mates with 'those in charge'.

CHEER UP, IT'S ALL IN A GOOD CAUSE

(SWEET BUT SOUR PORKER)

Other gods were responsible for things like the earth, dogs, millet, rice, you name it, but the god of the sky was the top god to whom all the others had to answer. The god that looked after the people on a daily basis was the god of the kitchen and he apparently reported to the god of the sky about what they'd been up to, once a year, on New Year's Eve. That's why the Chinese still make such a big deal of it.

Dead Nosy

The Chinese were also obsessed with the members of their family that had died (their ancestors), as they believed, rather daftly if you ask me, that they still had a big say in the well-being of those still living. In the Han period, especially, people became convinced that many of their ex-rellies were out to get 'em, and spent far too much of their time trying to suck up to them in every possible way. In each Chinese house was an ancestors' room where the oldies and deadies were supposed to live (or die). Poor old Mum, as well as looking after the ones that were still alive, was forever having to take the dead ones food as well. One can only suppose that the cat ate what she left out for them.

← SPECIAL POT FOR THE DEAD'S DINNERS

Always and Forever

The poor old Chinese were also fascinated by the avoidance of death for as long as possible (and who can blame them?). They believed that if they played their cards right, they could avoid their bodies becoming old and finally wearing out, which sounds rather attractive.* A good job to have had in Ancient China was that of a magician, who was not only supposed to have been able to get hold of the drugs (a kind of spiritual dealer), some of which contained ground-up gold or pearls, but also claimed to be in touch with all those who'd achieved immortality 'on the other side'. I don't get it: you're either dead or you're not in my book.

Useless Fact No. 637

One chap was so convinced these drugs would work, that he smeared his whole house, family, servants and pets with them so that they'd all live for ever with him. I should imagine (and hope) that it didn't work.

Emperors in the 2nd century BC often sent out large expeditions to the edges of the known world, to find where the immortals went after death (see Pointless Travel in Ancient Times). They sometimes came back a little crestfallen (but mostly didn't come back at all).

Yin and Yang

These sound like two characters out of Aladdin, but they were and still are very important to the Chinese way of life, especially in deciding what they eat and how they feel. According to the *very* Ancient Chinese, the creation of the world was due to two strong forces, which could still be

*A little bit late for you, Mr Farman. Ed

recognized on an everyday basis. Yin was associated with the female side – cold, dark and weak (no comment), and Yang, the male – warm, light and heavenly (of course)*. Apparently it depends on nature as to which is on the way up or on the way down and therefore how good a time you're going to have.

Famous Five

Fire, water, metal, wood and earth (the five elements) were created by Yin and Yang. They were powerful enough to decide what the material world would be like (sounds a bit like God to me).

The powers of the five elements were associated with other groups of five, like colours (green, red, black, white (a colour?), and yellow), directions (north, south, centre (a direction?), east and west), five sacred mountains, five musical instruments, five fingers on the hand (plus thumbs?), five toes on the foot . . . You understand?

The Point of It All

In order for mankind to be OK on earth it was important that the forces of Yin and Yang were in perfect balance. Certain members of those groups of five (directions, colours, etc.) could be used as allies in case it looked as if you might be heading for a natural disaster (getting your Yin Yangs in a twist) or even some big political punch-up. If the balance went severely wonky you could safely expect an earthquake, volcano, flood, famine, athlete's foot or *even worse*! That's why the first Chinese to settle in the Yellow River Valley tried their level best always to stay on the right side of nature.

*Sexist or what? Ed

Immortality Forever

Hold on, this is where it gets well wacky. Yin, Yang, and the Five Elements (sounds like a Chinese soul band) could all be combined with a way of living for ever. The white tiger – symbol of Metal and the Guardian of the West – sometimes shows the way to a heavenly world over which the Queen Mother of the West presides (I knew she was old, but not *that* old). Apparently, if mankind wanted a life of eternal bliss (sounds cool), there might well be winged dragons at his disposal to take him there (like heavenly mini-cabs?).

The symbol illustrating the balanced Yin and Yang goes a bit like this, by the way.

More . . .

As you might have guessed, there's a lot more to Yin and Yang than this, but if you want to know more, beware – you could be in for a long, complicated read, as well as a lot of very dodgy nosh, as Yin and Yang feature heavily in the preparation of Chinese food.

Taoism

As well as all that Yin and Yang business, another set of beliefs was being thought up by a few dead clever people at the end of the Han period. This was the aforementioned Taoism. *Tao* was the secret by which everything in the universe (and how it worked) could be understood, along with the best way a person could fit in with it. All clear?

The Taoist *religion* was slightly different, and mostly involved yet another way of trying to find a method of avoiding death. This pursuit was carried out by a few guys who reckoned they understood how it all worked (until, presumably, they died themselves). They got their patients to undergo a whole load of rites, take dodgy potions and plead forgiveness for their faults. If the patient requested something and it actually happened, then it was due to the master's secret powers (all rewards gratefully received). If it all went wrong, then, without doubt, it was down to the person not trying hard enough. Haven't we heard all that before?

One of their better 'tricks' was to take on the personality of a particular dead person (much used in spiritualism today). They regarded themselves as the masters (rather than the servants) of death. Sounds pretty spooky to me!

Buddhism

Buddhism crept into China from northern India via the merchants who were constantly traipsing up and down the Silk Road. Buddha was a real person and had in fact been a certain Mr Siddhartha (an Indian prophet from the 5th century BC). It seems he left home in tears because he couldn't bear the hardship of the peasants, or the fact that the plough his dad used occasionally chopped worms in half. (Odd, that – I didn't think that did them any harm! Simply made each half a new best friend.*)

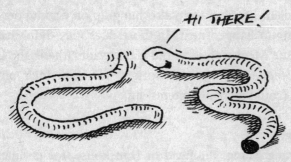

HI THERE!

Anyway, the religion was introduced to a society that firmly believed in ancestors, Heaven, the spirits of nature and, like the rest of them, a continual search for a way out of dying. Buddhism fitted in quite nicely as it forbade selfishness, ambition and an obsession with possessions. It also forbade lying, killing, stealing, going with someone else's missus, drinking too much and careless parking. While Buddhism hoped to free the body and soul from all the pain in the world, the Taoists had only really practised ways of preparing the poor old body as a home *fit* for a soul. Geddit? Best of all Buddhism cut right across social divisions – you didn't have to be rich to join.

*What *are* you talking about? Ed

The poorer Chinese of the Han Dynasty took to Buddhism like fish to chips,* and by AD 200 huge temples were being built with massive bronze statues of the Buddha ('the Enlightened One'). By T'ang time this new foreign religion was being followed by all sorts, including an intellectual called Hsuan-tsang who went off to India and translated loads of Buddhist works into Chinese, which was greatly appreciated when he got home.

Telling the Future
The Ancient Chinese were also hung up on finding out what was going to happen next. In those days they didn't have all our Mystic Megs or fairground clairvoyants (thank the Lord), so they tended to try and work it out from their physical features (could be really interesting).

Unlucky!
Take Wang Mang, the head of Han house, for instance. He was told, rather unflatteringly, by the court fortune-teller, that

he had the eyes of an owl, the jowl of a tiger and the bark of a jackal. Also that, although very capable of eating others, he was more than likely to get eaten himself (funny people, the Chinese).

*Shouldn't that be 'like a fish to water'? *Ed*

Wang Mang thanked the fortune-teller for the warning and then promptly killed him (the fortune-teller obviously hadn't predicted that, or he'd have kept his mouth shut). I think it's safe to assume Wang Mang hadn't believed the description of himself, but nevertheless, it was reported that he did refuse to see any dangerous-looking visitors (especially if they seemed a bit peckish).

Burial: Chinese Style

Death was all the rage in China – it became almost a national pastime. If your mum and dad died, you had to mourn them for three years and wear white (not black). It was a bit of a joke really, as people often looked after their mums and dads a lot better after they were dead than when the poor old codgers were alive.

The Chinese were convinced that their dead were going on to live in another, much better place (Slough?), and for that reason kings and emperors took all their favourite things to the tomb with them, including their rather hapless and rather dead courtiers who'd been swiftly executed (I bet they got a bit edgy when the boss got poorly). Luckily the First Emperor of China took life-size terracotta replicas of his whole army with him, which, although a relief for the real-life soldier lads, must have been a bit of a squeeze for the old Emp.

Posh Tombs

Noblemen's tombs had all mod cons and it was quite a shame that the occupant could only live in it while dead (if you see what I mean). The tombs were built above the ground (30 metres high in some cases), and had a magnificent sealed doorway, which led (or didn't lead, I suppose) into a massive entrance hall. This, in turn, led to another hall where the stiff would meet his dead visitors formally. Then there were storerooms and a fully equipped kitchen (for when he got hungry in the middle of the death). There would also be a little well in case he got thirsty.

Best of all, he'd have a kind of rumpus room where he and his spooky mates could party into eternity. All the main rooms would be painted with jolly scenes of the present resident and his ex-mates, to remind him of some of the good times they'd had in the past. Outside these rooms were big spaces for the storing of replica horses and real carriages. Some of these massive tombs, most times buried under monstrous mounds and crammed full of priceless artefacts and jewels, are still unexplored (for fear of bad luck) to this day.

Useless Fact No 639
The bodies of the dead-rich dead would be dressed in flash suits made of squares of jade, linked with golden wires which were supposed to preserve their bodies. Unfortunately theirs rotted just the same as anyone else's. Oh well, nice to know there are some things money just can't buy!

Poor Tombs
Common-folk like us (unless you, dear reader, are royalty or something*) had to be content with a small hole in the ground and paper cut-outs of their favourite things. False money was rather sensibly burned instead of the real stuff, and offered to the actual dead person about to go underground. Their name would then be added to a long list of all the other ex-members of the same family, which was engraved on a stone tablet.

*In which case they shouldn't be reading this sort of stuff. Ed

Poorer Tombs

If you were really poor, however, you'd just be chucked in a pit.
If you were unlucky as well as really poor and were a victim of
plague or famine, you'd probably just be left by the side of the
road to rot – or be dragged off and consumed by passing
animals. Is that a Chinese take-away?

꽃 *CHINESE ARMIES*
(or *The Han vs The Hun*)

Although the Chinese didn't go out on purpose to get into scraps with 'abroad', they were always trying to keep 'abroad' out of their land or else fighting amongst themselves. So much so, that all men between the ages of 22 and 56 would be expected, at sometime or other, to be in someone or other's army for a couple of years.

In the Han period, there could have been as many as a million men in the military service at any one time. The worst job, without any doubt, would have been to be posted to one of the far-flung garrisons on the edge of the Chinese Empire, away from their homes, families and pets. Most of the soldiers were infantry (foot soldiers) but to be in the cavalry was such an honour that the soldiers actually volunteered. They usually came from the posher end of society, which was just as well seeing as there was no pay.

Guess What?

● What would you do if you didn't want your next-door neighbour to trample your daffodils? You'd build a wall.

● What would you do if you didn't want strange people marching through your town? You'd build a wall.

● What would you do if you didn't want foreigners settling in your country? Well, you wouldn't build a wall, cos that would be far too expensive – unless, that is, you were Ancient Chinese. They were fed up with the Mongol horsemen of the Hsiung-Nu (who went on to be the Huns that caused the collapse of the Roman Empire) galloping willy-nilly through their lands, so decided to build a wall to keep 'em out. Not any old wall – oh no – but the longest, thickest, tallest, expensivest wall that had ever been built before or since.

The Great Wall

The Great Wall (as it was imaginatively called) stretched 1,400 miles from the Yellow Sea, to the Jade Gate, where the ancient Silk Road crossed into the massive wilderness of Central Asia. It was built mostly by convicts and about a million of them died during its construction.

Useless Fact No. 642

The Great Wall of China is the only man-made feature on our planet that can be observed from the moon. Apart from Prince Charles's ears . . .*

Did it Work?

Sort of. The trouble with a wall 1,400 miles long is that you have to have rather a lot of chaps guarding it just to make sure no one jumps over. Although they had 12-metre high watch-towers every 200 metres, it became almost impossible to man all of them at the same time, so the soldiers were always scurrying from one to the other when the hostile hordes appeared on the horizon.

*That's our future king you're talking about. Ed

Wall Work

The other function of the wall was to protect the lines of communication for diplomats or merchants' camel trains journeying out through Central Asia. The Great Wall was usually menned by mans* from villages up to six to eight weeks' march away.

As I said at the beginning of the book, the climate changes so much throughout China, that many of these travelling soldiers found themselves rather inappropriately dressed (and armed) when they reached the awesome, freezing mountain ranges, the wide, sweltering desert plains or the dense, tropical forests full of nasty, cross animals. Even the people they met along the way looked a bit odd as they got further and further away from home, and some of those they came across weren't from Chinese stock at all – and they didn't even speak the same lingo. Sounds like me in Scotland.

Tower Time

When the soldiers finally arrived at the wall, they'd split up and go to the various watchtowers that were along its length and in sight of each other. In order to communicate with the other towers, they'd raise flags or light fires (depending whether it was dark or not). Each tower grew its own food and reared its own animals.

On the 'foreign' side of the wall they would cunningly spread smooth sand banks so that they could check whether anyone had been creeping about at night. If anyone wanted to cross the wall, either way, they'd be questioned to make sure they weren't convicts, or enemies, or smugglers or estate agents.

*You must surely mean 'manned by men'? Ed

Lists

The Chinese army, like the rest of the Chinese people, were staggeringly efficient and crazy about lists. Lists of their servicemen – names, ages and where they came from, lists of their families, lists of the taxable property of the officers, lists of the particular performances of these officers, lists of all the signals, lists of the stores, lists of the official documents that passed by them, lists of the weapons they held at the fort, lists of the animals, lists of the sick, and so on, and so on, and . . .

What to Wear?

The Chinese army wore impressive outfits of leather and bronze. Their breastplates were made from lots of little squares of metal linked at the corners and worn over a leather tunic. Bronze helmets with a leather back bit protected their necks. Swords and powerful crossbows as well as evil-looking spears protected the rest of them. They had efficient harnesses to protect their horses and were the first to wear stirrups (a thousand years before Europeans) to protect their . . .*

*Thank you – we get the picture. Ed

Chapter 6

AWFULLY LAWFUL

Early Lawlessness

The first records of any laws in Ancient China (or most of the world, come to that) were in 536 BC in the state of Cheng. Before then there was no proper written-down list of what was or wasn't lawful. Can you imagine that? It meant that in most places, it was largely up to those in charge at any given time to decide who could do what to whom and when and why. Before proper laws were brought in, the Ancient Chinese were expected to abide by their own handed-down, self-imposed rules. The 'law' was a sort of unspoken promise to their fellow man, and they were continually reminded (quite painfully) if they let the side down.

DIY Law

Even after 536 BC, however, the state still relied a bit on the family to keep its members on the straight and narrow, and would seldom question any punishment dished out provided it was severe enough. Obviously, if the things they did were *really* awful the state would step in. Punishments ranged from light floggings and fines, through to slicing into tiny pieces (for three or more murders), with beheading and strangulation somewhere in between. Strangulation was the most popular way to be executed, because it meant you at least kept your body in one piece – which the spirits apparently found easier to inhabit when you were dead (I don't think I'd care!).

Top Ten Popular Family Laws and Punishments

一 If a son struck a parent it was off with his head – certainly more effective than being sent to bed with no supper.

二 If he simply shouted at his parents it would be strangulation by Dad. How many times would *you* be dead by now?

I TAKE IT HE WON'T BE NEEDING THIS SCARF

三 If a parent struck his son it was fine – unless the kid died, and then Dad might be given a light punishment.

四 The punishment for hitting your elder brother or sister was two years' imprisonment. Blimey, I'd have been in prison throughout my childhood. If you broke their tooth, finger, toe or rib it was banishment far from home. If a sharp instrument was used, or if a limb was broken, or an eye blinded, it was strangulation (or beheading if the victim died).

五 A wife could expect 100 strokes of the *zhang* (a long heavy stick) if she hit her husband, and she'd be strangled if she injured him.

六 A husband, as you might have guessed, could beat his missus as much as he liked, but if he actually injured her it was 100 strokes and a severe ticking-off.

七 Parents-in-law were quite free to kill their daughter-in-law if they could provide a good enough reason for doing so. Like skin on the rice pudding?

八 Marrying or having an affair with a relative, or even someone with the same surname, was punishable by death.

九 If a dad was sentenced to death, his son was perfectly free to take his place and be executed instead. How d'you fancy that, lads?

千 A son or daughter could on no account choose their own husband or wife. If they got secretly engaged they could expect a jolly good zhanging.

New Crimes for Old

When the new state laws arrived there was a bit of an outcry. The people thought that these laws could never deal properly with the wide range of the bad things that they could think up. By making laws about just a few specific crimes, they thought it would (and did) invite people to invent a whole load of other wicked things that weren't covered. In other words, it put ideas into their heads. The alternative to this was to have just one judge who listened to every case and decided who was or wasn't guilty, and what should happen to them.

Judge and Jury

This latter idea seemed to work OK at first. Each aristocrat set himself up as judge and jury, and was only answerable to the nobleman above him. Mostly, however, a lot of the more petty crimes (bad rickshaw parking, etc.) were still dealt with by the families themselves as a matter of honour. So, if young Jimmy pinched something from another family, he would be tried and punished by his elder rellies, and if his dad pinched something, he'd be tried and punished by *his* elder rellies.

The main point behind all this* is that whoever was doing the judging when the new laws came in had to be seen to be perfectly honest – and this, dear reader, is where all the problems began. The thing to remember about the Ancient Chinese was that those in charge were always easy to bribe, and any kind of justice could be swayed by how much you could shell out (money, jobs, gifts, beautiful daughters, etc.). The Emperor, admittedly, was constantly warning his underlings against such dangers, but China was a one heckuva big place and he obviously couldn't be everywhere at once.

Be Warned
Even so, when they put their minds to it they could think up some pretty gruesome punishments – like cutting off toes, slicing off ears, pulling out tongues, lopping off noses (for the not-so-serious stuff), and, for a particular nasty murder, nothing short of boiling the accused alive seemed appropriate. Punishments were especially severe in the army. If a charioteer, for instance, had a couple of troublesome horses, who pulled their master out of line, he could expect to be executed on the spot. (What about the horses?)

I SUPPOSE IT WAS OUR FAULT REALLY

EX BOSS

*There is a point? Oh goodie. Ed

Rich go Free

As usual, the rich and powerful got away with most things, because a) predictably, there were few people who dared tell the rich and powerful what to or what not to do, and b) they usually had a private army to make sure no one even tried. Mind you, if anyone did manage to bring them to justice, very often their whole family would be executed, or made into slaves, for good measure. I think I'd have been a trifle miffed if a member of my family caused me to be enslaved (let alone be killed).

WAS IT SOMETHING I DID?

Life or Death

Murder in very Ancient China had always been frowned on, but was only seen as a crime if someone of greater power saw it that way and, more to the point, decided to do something about it. The *law,* as I said, had simply not existed before 536 BC, and human life was dirt cheap. For instance, a minister of the state of Chin, Chao Hsuan-tzu, used his influence to have a guy called Han Hsien-tzu put in charge of military discipline. To see whether Han could do the job, Chao waited for the next battle (every ten minutes in those days). He ordered one of his soldiers to break out of line, which the poor chap obediently did. Han promptly had him arrested and executed, even though he was one of his new boss's personal guards. Chao praised Han for his commendable discipline, even though he'd ordered the poor bloke to do it. As for the soldier – tough!

A Dog's Life

If a nobleman's food was thought to have been poisoned, or was 'off', it was fed to a servant or a dog (same thing). If they died it was declared unsafe. The same sort of wacky logic can be seen in the story of the girl-servant of the wife of the future emperor of China, who once overheard a rather juicy conversation of her master's and reported it to her mistress. The girl, bless her, was praised for her loyalty and then, rather unfairly, executed, purely so that she wouldn't tell anyone else.

These killings of commoners weren't done out of any class hatred but just what one did to solve a minor problem or irritation. Simple but effective! Assassinations were also two a penny, as often it was the only way of getting someone out of a job. Life, as I said before, was very cheap up China way.

Useless Fact No. 645
Many of the laws and punishments developed in ancient times were still in use right up to the end of China's Imperial Age in 1911. But I still wouldn't risk shouting at your Dad . . .

Chapter 7

ELYTS ESENIHC - GNITIRW

Everyone knows that Chinese writing goes from back to front and bottom to top and is made up of funny little squiggly pictures. But how did it all come about?

Good Question
The first Chinese writing ever found was on animal bones and tortoise shells dating back to 1500 BC and was apparently questions written, rather pointlessly I'd have thought, by the Shang kings to their ancestors (like 'What do these funny little squiggly pictures mean?').

Each picture, it turned out, had a meaning, and combinations of these pictures changed these meanings into new meanings (if you know what I mean). The little symbols could represent actual things like pigs or porcupines, or abstract things like joy or grumpiness. If, for instance, you put the drawing of the sun together with that of the moon, the new image would mean 'brightness', or if you put two tree symbols together it would mean 'forest' (a pretty weedy forest, in my opinion). What do you think would happen if you put two rabbit symbols together? Answers on a postcard.

Gradually, as the years passed, the symbols began to look less and less like what they were originally meant to represent, until they arrived at today's style of writing – beautiful, but totally incomprehensible (unless you're Chinese). Just to make

SUN SHEEP HORSE FIELD

WATER TREE BIRD BURGER

things even more confusing, they later made up several ways of writing the same word. Help!

Character Play

At the time of the First Emperor there were 3,300 standard characters which were for everyone to use. During the Han Dynasty, they realized it might be quite handy if every district wrote in the same style. So a standard text was engraved on stone tablets that were to be saved for ever and ever (amen). The project was started in AD 175; it took 8 years' hard sweat (and a lot of chipping) to complete the 50 stones. Scholars flocked to the capital city, where the tablets were kept, to take copies of them (like brass rubbings) on the newly invented paper.

Those old calligraphers had obviously got carried away, for the number of characters swelled to 10,000 even though, right to this day, most ordinary people can only get their brains round 2–3,000 (which I reckon's pretty good going). In those distant days only a few select people knew how to read and write, anyway.

Useless Fact No. 647

The style that was brought into use during the Han period only went out of fashion at the end of the Imperial Age in 1911. Even so, it's very similar today.

A Bit Fishy

For centuries the Chinese wrote on wooden strips, bone or long pieces of silk with a brush or bamboo 'pen', until, as I just mentioned, in about AD 105 some clever-clogs went and invented proper paper, from pounded-up old rags, bark or fishing nets.* This opened the whole literature business up and soon scrolls and books were created. They were treated with awe and respect and were handed down through the generations.

Early Graffiti

In those early days writing was mostly used to record the fine (but boring) lives and achievements of government officials, to flatter the emperor and also to record building contracts (which were often scrawled on the walls of the buildings in question). Tricky when it fell down...

In 26 BC the Han emperor of the day asked for every bit of writing (on silk presumably), including the sayings of various of the philosophers, to be collected from all the districts and assembled in the city. A massive imperial library was built and it is because of this amazing collection that many of these texts still exist.

*Are you sure about the fishing nets? Ed
Yes, I'm sure I've read it somewhere. JF

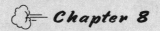

Chapter 8

BIRTH, MARRIAGE... *AND DIVORCE*

As we have seen on the telly recently, baby girls are a real no-no in China, and always have been. Boys were fab; they kept the family name going and could do all the heavy work on the family farms. Many baby girls (apparently up to a third) were thrown in rivers, buried alive or just left by the roadside to be eaten by dogs or wild pigs, especially if they had anything even slightly wrong with them. Poor people saw absolutely no problem, emotional or otherwise, in disposing of their babies in order to have one less mouth to feed.

SORRY KIDS - ONLY ENOUGH FOR FOUR. WHICH ONE GOES?

Useless Fact No. 650

One kindly emperor was known to send a cart round the walls of his immense castle every morning to collect the daily crop of abandoned girls and take them to a special temple where nurses would look after them.

The alternative to murder or abandonment was to sell your daughter as soon as she was old enough to be a prostitute, slave, concubine (spare wife), or supermarket check-out girl.

Getting Hitched

Marriage was regarded as all a woman was fit for: her only true destiny. The age seems to vary, but at the beginning of the 5th century BC it was decreed in the state of Yueh that all men had to be married by the age of 20 and women by 17. If a young man or woman didn't manage to get hitched by that age, it wasn't them who were punished, but their parents for not arranging it (which is fair when you consider that the poor kids had no choice in the matter anyway).

Concubines

Many young girls in their early teens were sold as concubines. A rich Chinese man could have as many girls as he liked (or could afford) in his house-hold. This was very popular if a man's

wife couldn't produce kids (or should I say, boys) or if he just fancied a change. Mind you, he couldn't treat his real wife as a concubine, as the penalty was 100 strokes of the old zhang, and likewise he couldn't treat his favourite concubine as a wife for fear of 90 strokes.

It's a bit weird, but the poor girls were expected to treat the guy's wife as a mother, and were protected from the advances of other men by very strict laws.

Splitting Up

When it came to who could or couldn't divorce, the position of the poor old wife was dead dodgy. Legally there were what was known as the 'Seven Outs', which were:

一 If she couldn't produce nippers (most feared amongst young wives).

二 Flirting with other men.

三 Neglect of the in-laws.

四 Rowdiness.

五 Theft.

六 Jealousy and speaking badly of people.

七 Incurable disease.

Most of these, I'm sure you'll agree, were rather unfair (especially the mother-in-law bit). As for kicking the poor dear out if she got severely ill, that really *was* charming!

On the other hand there were the 'Three Not Outs', which meant she *couldn't* be divorced if:

- She'd kept up the three years decreed mourning for either of her in-laws.
- Her husband's family had become rich after she'd married into it.
- She had no home to return to.

Pawning

You'll like this one, girls. If a husband didn't want to get rid of his wife altogether, he could consider pawning her (selling her to someone else for a given amount of time and then buying her back at the end of the period). This was extremely popular if a husband was a bit strapped for cash, but didn't want to lose his missus altogether. Neat idea, eh?*

Useless Fact No. 651
Speaking of which, the first coin in China was called the *cash*.

HOW MUCH FOR A COUPLE OF DAYS?

*No comment. Ed

Nun the Worse

With all this going on, you'd have thought that divorce was always on the wife's mind, but, as you might have guessed, it didn't work the other way round . . . If she simply left home, she could be dragged back, imprisoned for two years, given 100 lashes, or sold to the highest bidder. If she married someone else when away, she could be strangled. Whatever the reason for the divorce, she couldn't survive that well as her family would rarely have her back (what would the neighbours say?) and no respectable man would have her either. Her choices were limited and not that appealing: begging, prostitution, suicide or – worst of all – becoming a nun.

Getting Even

The only way for women in Ancient China to achieve any kind of equality was to have loads of sons, or to hang in there until she was old. Old women were treated with enormous veneration as the family heads. Unfortunately, if a woman had no sons, she was doomed in this life and the next. She could not be an 'ancestress' and that meant that her soul would have no means of support when dead.

On the whole then, girls, Ancient China doesn't seem to be the sort of place to go if you're into time travel . . .

Chapter 9

DRUGS, NEEDLES AND NONSENSE: CHINESE MEDICINE

One of the awkward things about being a criminal* in Ancient China, was that there was a fair chance that you could end up on the chopping block, having all your entrails pulled out and measured with little bamboo sticks, or your body cut into little pieces by a skilled butcher while being watched by a load of students.

It was all done in the name of the Chinese pursuit of knowledge, and much of what was discovered all those centuries ago by the doctors/magicians has become dead fashionable today (especially with the brown rice and sandals brigade). The most famous book, written during the T'ang dynasty, was called *The T'ang Book of Drugs and Herbs*, and is like a bible to this day. It concentrated on medicines that came from plants and rocks, along with acupuncture (the sticking of needles), moxibustion (the burning of the herb *Artemesia moxa* just at the point of pain), diet, massage and small incisions. They also found out a lot about sick people from taking their pulse (see the bit on acupuncture). In AD 200 another book came out describing most of the best infectious diseases (including the big one, typhoid) with suggestions of how to cure them. They also invented a rather groovy anaesthetic by mixing cannabis with wine (dead trendy).

*I thought this chapter was about medicine? Ed
OK, give us a chance! JF

Ancient Chinese Remedies

One of the weirdest ones was for concussion or a severe blow to the head – and it was used until relatively recently (17th century). It went something like this:

Dunk said head into
iced water.

Wrap head tightly, each end being
pulled as hard as possible by two
strong men.

Strike patient on head
with large piece of wood.

You might be dead, but at least you didn't have a headache or concussion any more.

As for other remedies, if you visited the doc in Ancient China, you might expect any of the following:

⌒ DISLOCATED RIBS

The patient would be held between two assistants, and a bowl of iced water would be chucked over his or her chest. The resulting sharp intake of breath was supposed to make the rib spring back into place (ouch!).

⇒ SPRAINS AND INJURIES

The early European idea of putting injured patients to bed with the minimum of movement was frowned on by the Ancient Chinese, who believed that gentle exercise and fasting prevented the blood from settling anywhere it shouldn't. Ten out of ten to China: this is now standard procedure throughout the world.

≡ FEVERISH COLDS

Take ten parts of Wu Hui with ten parts of Chu. Mix with six parts of Hsi Hsin and four parts of Kuei, in boiling water. The resulting instant bowel movement and uncontrollable urinating was reckoned to have the patient better by morning. I think I'd rather stick with the cold.

⁇ KORO ALERT!!!

The Chinese male was and still is totally obsessed with his virility and ability to make little Chinese males. Mention the word Koro or Shook Yong in any Chinese circles and you can watch the blood drain from the men's faces. This is (and was) a condition (almost certainly mythical) which, if contracted, was supposed to make the penis retract into the abdomen and, if not caught in time, disappear altogether with fatal consequences. Men who think they have this disease walk around holding onto their willy for grim death or tying it up with string or rubber bands, clamping it with metal clamps, chopsticks or even clothes pegs (what about a bulldog clip?)*. Needless to say, injuries resulting from this treatment were far worse than anything that the disease (if it ever existed) could possibly have caused.

Useless Fact No. 653

As late as 1967 there was a widespread rumour in China that Koro was caused by eating pigs vaccinated against swine fever. Apparently, pork sales ground to a halt throughout the country.

Taking the Needle (Acupuncture)

The world's very oldest medical textbook was called something like *The Emperor's Classic Book of Internal Medicine*. It was written over 4,500 years ago and contains the first record of the use of needles as a way of curing all illnesses. It goes something like this.

Yin and Yang, as described earlier, composed the whole world (according to the Chinese), and when a person is healthy the two are in perfect balance. When you get ill, they fall out of balance, and some bits of the body have too much

---

* This can't be true. You're making it up. Ed
If you don't believe me, read a book by a learned Chinese chap
called Chong, pages 640–641. JF

Yin or too much Yang. By putting little needles into different parts of the 12 meridians (the rivers of energy in the body) it either blocks off or stimulates the flow. The 12 meridians are connected to different organs, which means that even if you stick a needle in someone's big toe, it can still affect somewhere completely different (the liver in this case).

Each wrist has six pulses, each of which are in turn connected to a meridian. (Are you still with me?) An expert acupuncturist is supposed to be able to detect an illness from these alone (and any that might be on the way). Modern needles are made of steel with little electrical pulses running through them, but in the olden days they used simple needles of wood or stone. Ow! Acupuncture is still the world's most ancient and mysterious treatment, and I and the whole staff of Macmillan Children's Books strongly recommend that you do not, on any account, try anything remotely like this at home (not even on the dog).*

*I agree – for once. Ed

Chapter 10

CHINESE HIGH JINKS

In those days, your average bottom-of-the-pile Chinese peasants never had much of a good time as, a) they were far too busy working, and b) they made precious little extra loot to have a good time with. Life for the better-off, like the better-off everywhere, was therefore . . . better.*

In the local marketplaces, your average nobleman could lounge about sipping tea or wine, watching a whole army of performers, from story-tellers to acrobats, musicians to fire-eaters. During festivals the acts would go on all day.

The Chinese have always loved games, including anything to do with gambling. Cock-fighting was their favourite, along with cards, dice and strange games like Double Sixes, the rules of which have long been forgotten. Gambling, it must be said, was frowned upon by the authorities, as it was seen as a way of making money without giving any contribution to society.

Kite-u-Like

The Chinese have always been fascinated by kites, probably because they invented them, and indeed they made the very best. They also loved all ball games and a kind of badminton, which is odd because the English say *they* invented it in 1860. The big cities had lovely parks where the town's folk would have picnics or simply stroll about looking at each other.

*Really? Ed

Rich Pickings

The rich would have almost continous entertainment at home. They would probably have had their own personal musicians playing that plinky-plonky (to our ears) music you hear in Chinese restaurants, calling in the bands of travelling magicians, acrobats, sword-fighters and wrestlers as and when they needed them. Poets, of course, would be expected to make their rhymes up on the spot. They even had tiger-fighting in the back yard on special occasions.

An emperor's party would go on all night, even though he'd be expected to get up early in the morning (not much point being an emperor, if you're not allowed a lie-in).

On nice days, the wealthy Chinese would go out to watch horse and dog racing or do a bit of bird-hunting in the huge parks that were reserved just for them. All the poor could do was pee* longingly over the walls from the sprawling slums that surrounded them.

Grub's Up

It is said that where our fellow creatures are concerned, if it moves, the Chinese will eat it. (But then, they probably find our taste in food rather odd too. Lamb with redcurrant jelly?) In Ancient China, it seemed, no animal was safe. Even the family dog had to behave himself otherwise he'd be in the pot before you could say dog-suey.

Useless Fact No. 656

If you've ever seen the Chow Chow, that magnificent hound with the purple tongue that looks like a great ball of fur... Well, the Ancient Chinese were known to eat it. Chow mein?

*I think you're missing an 'r' at the end of that word. Ed

Pets' Corner

If one of the master's camels was looking a little knackered,
they'd chop his feet off and eat them
as a great delicacy.

Sharks would lose their fins, fish would lose their lips, and not
only did the Chinese eat every type of bird that flew, they even
made soup out of the poor little devils' nests.* Bear-hunting
was a great sport for the rich and if they got one, everyone
would be asked back for a Bear-B-Cue. (Sorry!) The favourite
bit was, like the camel, the paw, which I'd have thought would
be a bit yukky. Bear paws – no thank you.

So What's New?

The Chinese city dwellers simply sat back and waited for the
country peasants to provide them with food, even though the
peasants hardly had enough to eat themselves. A peasant's
normal diet would be a bowl of stewed vegetables with millet
(if they lived in the north) or rice (if they didn't). The
vegetables they favoured were bamboo shoots, lotus roots and
those special very green greens they always have in Chinese
restaurants.

*Birds' Nest Soup is *not* made out of birds' nests. Ed

Useless Fact No. 659

Chopsticks go way back into Ancient Chinese history. Have you ever tried to use them? It's like playing the piano with rubber gloves on.* Don't panic, however, most Chinese simply use them to scoop their food into their mouths directly from the bowl.

Party Time

The wealthy Ancient Chinese always loved parties and banquets and the more rare and therefore expensive the dishes, the better.

Servants in beautiful flowing robes would scurry backwards and forwards from the kitchens where the many chefs (sometimes hundreds) would be chopping and mincing, hacking and frying, boiling and stewing and straining and baking at fever pitch.

A Chinese banquet consisted of loads of courses and was served with a delicious and easy-to-get-drunk-on rice wine.

Useless Fact No. 660

Grapes only came along in the Han Dynasty, along with tea, which quickly became China's favourite tipple.

Sexy Food

The Chinese have always believed that certain foods and substances are a great help in the old bedroom department (as most of the hornless rhinos will tell you). Aphrodisiacs included distilled urine, extracts from the glands of bears, goats and bulls, and the droppings of any animals that were noted for their fierceness (lions, eagles, hamsters, etc.). I don't know about you, but I think that stuff just might put me off the whole business.

---

*Why on earth would you play the piano with rubber gloves on? Ed
To see what it's like eating with chopsticks, of course JF

NICE SOUP. WHAT IS IT?

Soup Recipe

One of their favourites for a cold night was dried stag's penis soup. Here's the recipe:

一 Take one large healthy stag (dead or alive).

二 Take one very sharp knife and approach stag carefully.

三 Cut—*

*Thank you, Mr Farman, but I think we've run out of space for this chapter. What a shame. Ed

TIME'S UP

Ah well, that's another great civilization dealt with in sixty odd pages.* If, by any chance, there are any areas that I haven't covered – sorry, but I've run out of words. (Anyway, there are loads of big, boring books on the subject, if you really haven't had enough.) And you can't really complain – let's face it, for the price of this book you couldn't even get a bowl of rice and a few sweet and sour pork balls.

However, if you'd like another course, why not try one of the other mighty works in this series? Don't go through them too quickly, however – I've still got to write the blinking things.

*Very odd pages, if you ask me. Ed